UPSIDE DOWN LIVING

technology

[
The Upside-Down Living series emphasizes living out
one's Christian faith through the lens of Jesus
by following values that seem so countercultural
they appear to be upside down.
]

Becca J. R. Lachman

Herald Press
Harrisonburg, Virginia

Technology
Upside-Down Living series

© 2016 by Herald Press, Harrisonburg, Virginia 22802
    All rights reserved.
International Standard Book Number: 978-1-5138-0155-1
Printed in United States of America

Written by Becca J. R. Lachman
Design by Merrill Miller
Cover photo by Zsolt Bicz/iStockphoto/Thinkstock/composite image

Unless otherwise noted, Scripture text is quoted, with permission, from the
New Revised Standard Version, © 1989, Division of Christian Education of the
National Council of Churches of Christ in the United States of America.

Some Scripture taken from *The Message*. © 2002. Used by permission of
NavPress Publishing Group.

For orders or information, call 1-800-245-7894 or visit HeraldPress.com.

20 19 18 17 16   10 9 8 7 6 5 4 3 2 1

NICOELNINO/ISTOCKPHOTO/THINKSTOCK/COMPOSITE IMAGE

[Contents]

Introduction 5

1. And They'll Know We Are Christians
   by Our Feed:
   Technology and Identity. 7

2. Be Still, and Know . . .
   Technology, Trust, and Control 13

3. Can You Hear Me Now?
   Technology and Community 19

4. Texts, Truth, and the Temple:
   Technology and the Body-Mind
   Connection 25

5. Ripples in the Water:
   Technology and Earth Care 31

6. I Can Make Peace with That:
   Technology and 21-st Century
   Peacemaking 37

About the Writer 45

[Introduction]

For many of us, decisions about technology happen hourly. Our vehicles, workplaces, homes, churches, communities, even our bodies, carry our choices. But what influences these decisions? For some it's profession or economic status. For others our choices relate to our health or location.

Without humans, technology is . . . well, *what is it?* Do we define and control technology, or does technology define and control us?

The question is as old as fire or the wheel. This study aims to add another layer—how might Christians talk together about technology? What might technology use look like when living out our faith through the lens of Jesus, whose own values seem so countercultural that they appear to be upside down? How might this upside-down living look in a household, neighborhood, congregation, country, and world—one life and one tablet at a time? Shouldn't the church community's input about technology be a vital part of our discernment?

This guide has six sessions organized into distinct themes. Many questions and ideas in one session could easily overlap with those in another. This study can't cover everything related to faith and technology; it's up to you to highlight the missing questions and resources, and to keep the dialogue going.

For this study, define *technology* as whatever forms of technology you and yours use most. On many days, for example, I spend 10–12 hours connected to screens on phones, tablets, or laptops. I allow them to be (or do they have to be?) the center of my work life, social life, and creative life, communicating with friends and mentors across the globe.

Please keep in mind that I am middle-class and nearing middle age, a white woman who is yet to be a parent. This all matters. My hope is that these pages also offer *you* a safe springboard to add your own questions and experiences to share with each other. This conversation needs you.

So let's keep seeking—not to simply dismiss or distrust—but to be awake. Technology's real power and potential aren't going any-where. Modern technology is a gift and, in many ways, a privilege. But most of all it's a tool we get to decide how to use, and I believe that for this great joy and responsibility, we need each other.

—Becca J. R. Lachman

1: AND THEY'LL KNOW WE ARE CHRISTIANS BY OUR FEED
[Technology and Identity]

[Rarely does the church community talk about technology, whether how it is used during worship or how individuals use it in their work or personal lives.]

[It's time to change that.]

If we are God's hands and feet today, then those hands navigate everything from steering wheels to search engines, and our feet make digital footprints. Sometimes those hands and feet choose to stay most connected with virtual communities, maybe to remind them of who they want to be.

With more platforms and ways of communicating than ever, are we proclaiming a Jesus-centered life more effectively?

> ⟦ **Is technology helping our identity in God to thrive?** ⟧

If we define what we worship as whatever we spend the most time, energy, and money on, then many North Americans would have to say they worship their devices. According to the United Nations, more people today have access to cell phones than toilets.[1] Some would point out that such a statistic is human progress, and that knowledge is transformative and life changing. And indeed, it can be.

Other contemporary voices, like writer Nicholas Carr, caution that the Internet has literally changed how our minds function: our brains have been rewired around interruption, satisfaction, and multitasking, rather than contemplation.[2] Do you even still remember the sentence you just read?

American teens spend upwards of nine hours per day on video games, online video streaming, and social media, according to a 2015 Common Sense Media study,[3] while the average American adult spends over 11 hours a day on electronic media.[4]

---

1 Teresa Welsh, "More Have Access to Cell Phones Than Toilets," *U.S. News and World Report*, November 18, 2014, http://www.usnews.com/news/blogs/data-mine/2014/11/18/on-un-world-toilet-day-more-have-access-to-cell-phones-than-toilets.
2 *The Shallows: What the Internet Is Doing to Our Brains* (New York: W. W. Norton, 2011).
3 "Landmark Report: U.S. Teens Use an Average of Nine Hours of Media Per Day," Common Sense Media, November 3, 2015, https://www.commonsensemedia.org/about-us/news/press-releases/landmark-report-us-teens-use-an-average-of-nine-hours-of-media-per-day.
4 "The Total Audience Report: Q4, 2014," Nielsen, March 11, 2015, http://www.nielsen.com/us/en/insights/reports/2015/the-total-audience-report-q4-2014.html.

Americans use electronic media 11+ hours a day

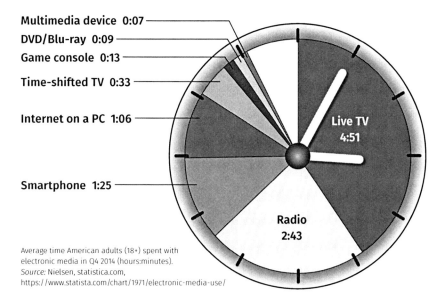

Multimedia device 0:07
DVD/Blu-ray 0:09
Game console 0:13
Time-shifted TV 0:33
Internet on a PC 1:06
Smartphone 1:25
Live TV 4:51
Radio 2:43

Average time American adults (18+) spent with electronic media in Q4 2014 (hours:minutes).
Source: Nielsen, statistica.com,
https://www.statista.com/chart/1971/electronic-media-use/

How might this affect self-expression and self-esteem when it comes to class, race, body image, and sexuality, not to mention spiritual identity?

A study in *Psychology Today* details that as technology has advanced and more people use it, the way we develop our identities has moved from being more internal to mostly external.[5] Because of the opportunity to be constantly digitally connected, where we are usually rated by our peers and perfect strangers alike, we are also asked to perform, collect, and carefully edit our digital selves.

[From podcasts and wikis to online journals and documentaries, technology offers Christians a powerful set of tools to be active salt and light in today's world.]

---

5   Jim Taylor, "Technology: Is Technoloyg Stealing Our (Self) Identities?" *Pyschology Today*, July 27, 2011, https://www.psychologytoday.com/blog/the-power-prime/201107/technology-is-technology-stealing-our-self-identities.

And yet through technology there are more ways than ever to search for clues about who we are as human beings and children of God.

The Internet offers:

- ongoing education
- conversation
- community identity

Facebook groups, blogs, church services posted as podcasts, and websites give us access to each other's stories. We confess to each other online, and we profess our forgiveness and the dancing of the Holy Spirit in our lives. As people of faith we are growing interactive, intergenerational branches in our digital family trees.

> **Do I fear that I won't exist or matter without a credit card or a Facebook account?**

Yet for those who have experienced identity theft, it can feel as if nothing is safe or sacred anymore. On some days, I wonder about other, more subtle versions of identity theft when it comes to the roles that technology sometimes plays in my life. Can a jubilant identity in Christ coexist with my robust digital identities?

Our digital world has also been redefining both language and the ways in which we interact with social systems: consider words including *friends*, *MySpace*, *feed*, and *community*. We might consider how our technology choices may be transforming words and practices like worship, Sabbath, or communion.

> **"For where two or three are gathered in my name, I am there among them" (Matthew 18:20).**

Is God with us in Google? Has Google become a kind of god? And can God work through our digital identities?

> "The fruit of the Spirit is love, joy, peace, patience, kindness, generosity, faithfulness, gentleness, and self-control" (Galatians 5:22-23).

Think about how technology intersects with the fruit of the Spirit—for good or bad. How might technology use better enable us to live out the fruit of the Spirit, or how might technology make such living more difficult? Consider the types of technology you and your communities use most on a daily basis, and in what ways they might fit into a contemporary telling of the Sermon on the Mount, specific to technology:

> "Blessed are those who [mine for the minerals that go into my laptop], for theirs is the kingdom of heaven . . ."

[Talk about It]

Technology and ourselves

▶ Consider defining what you worship as whatever you spend the most time, money, and energy on. Make a time chart for a week and track your time as honestly as possible.

	Sunday	Monday	Tuesday	Wednesday	Thursday	Friday	Sa
Work							
Sleep							
Transportation							
Eat							
TV							
Facebook							
Fantasy FB							
Texting							

Technology and others

▶ How do we witness technology influencing or shaping self-identity in people we love from different age groups?

▶ What assumptions do we carry when it comes to technology and others' identities?

▶ What might the technology we use most say about us?

Technology and discernment

▶ What is your current process for making decisions about technology use? Has it been helpful and effective? If not, what realistic steps could you take in order to try something new?

▶ If you could talk more about technology as it relates to your faith, where, or to whom, might you turn?

2 · BE STILL, AND KNOW . . .
Technology, Trust, and Control

For as long as I can remember, my dad has displayed handwritten messages to ponder on the refrigerator door. Most times, these are quotes gleaned from his reading life, centered among family photos and artwork by grandchildren. If I want to know how he is feeling about the world, these posted messages often give me a clue.

When I first saw this list, I gave my dad a hard time, teasing him about having a martyr complex. But then, something happened—the list wouldn't get out of my head, partly because so many things in my daily life seemed to be trying to convince me of the opposite. I *am* in control and important. Life *isn't* supposed to be so hard. Right?

> For the past few years, this has been the highlighted list on my parents' fridge:
>
> 1. Life is not fair.
> 2. Life is hard.
> 3. It's not about me.
> 4. I am going to die.

This list still makes my stomach flop, but I more fully understood why internalizing its truths daily might be so important, not only for my father, an intensive care unit nurse in his 60s, but for any of us who identify as a follower of Jesus.

Those who work in the medical field may encounter a human need for control more than some of us. Such people are trained to discern and use technology that has allowed us, in many cases, to live longer, healthier, and happier lives.

But as patients and family members, we can also bring assumption, privilege, and unrealistic expectation into our clinics and hospitals.

[**Quite simply, we want answers.**]

We want quick, cost-effective healing. We want to slow or even avoid disease, aging, pain, and death. Going to the Internet to research our symptoms can lead us down a rabbit hole—but can also empower us to know which questions to ask and what the options are.

In faith communities, technology has become an important and effective tool. We use it to plan worship and as a public relations tool to tell others about the good news. Because of technology, we can take control of shaping and sharing our faith and stories more than ever before. This is no small thing, especially for those who are marginalized or silenced, both inside and outside the church. But are there still spaces where we feel it's unethical or rude to use our devices? Is church one of them?

Indeed, technology choices might sometimes blur the boundaries we've practiced between need and want, or knowledge and wisdom. Who needs the metaphor of the lost sheep in a world where we can microchip our pets so they never are lost?

[**Many people use mobile devices during worship services to look up songs and Bible verses. Still others use them to fact-check the sermon. But what about those who respond to text messages during worship. Is that crossing the line?**]

So when do we stop being the master of technology and when, instead, does technology starts being the master of us? We use it to track an online purchase

that we know will arrive on our doorstep days later. We use it to incessantly checking weather apps. We use it to monitor our daily steps thanks to activity trackers. But all this makes me wonder: Are we weakening our willingness to surrender to God?

We often read Psalm 46:10 as an affirmation, but it is also a command:

[**"Be still, and know that I am God!**
I am exalted among the nations,
I am exalted in the earth."]

The Message expresses a related thought in Psalm 46:1: "God is a safe place to hide, ready to help when we need him."

Likewise, Psalm 37:7 asks us to "be still before the Lord, and wait patiently for him; do not fret over those who prosper in their way."

How do we interpret these verses in our contemporary lives, where government and business surveillance, corporate greed, and drone warfare are, for many of us, persistent but distant hums in the background of our living? Are we really being still if the house is quiet in the evening while we are scrolling on Facebook?

Sometimes, *being still* seems laughable. When we want answers, want to feel safe, or want to hide, where do we turn? I am surely not alone in saying that more often than I would like to admit, I reach for tools that let me explore knowledge on my own, or that numb feelings, or that allow me to avoid contemplation.

> **Yet the Bible is filled with invitations to feel God's presence.**

With this transformative love, to work toward upside-down living, God is waiting for us to show up to our regular dinner date with the divine, so to speak. God has the table booked; there are two glasses, two plates, and two sets of silverware.

As we increase our everyday technology use for things like communication, entertainment, identity building, and work productivity, we also need to be able to settle into real rest and inner peace. Sometimes that means using our devices and screens, but it also means setting them aside. This is easier said than done for many of us who might find it challenging to **take a technology Sabbath once a week**, let alone a true, unplugged vacation. Many American workers do not take all the vacation time owed them by their employer. Of those who take vacations, many fear losing business and so they feel obligated to check email while away. (You could still take your smartphone on vacation but turn your email off.)

Proverbs 3:5-6 says: "Trust in the Lord with all your heart, and do not rely on your own insight. In all your ways acknowledge him, and he will make straight your paths."

[Talk about It]

Technology and ourselves

▶ What types of technology help you feel in control of your daily living?

▶ Has technology helped you to more fully feel, or live out, the Holy Spirit's nudging? If so, in what ways?

▶ Do you feel there are acceptable and unacceptable places and situations to use certain technology? Do these boundaries reflect who you are as a person of faith? Explain.

Technology and others

▶ Should we check in with our pastors about their technology use? For example, do they feel they have to answer every call, every text or email, no matter the time or setting? Do we expect them to do this? Should we be helping them to embrace technology Sabbaths, too?

> This doesn't mean that we can't ever use a search engine again, but perhaps it can remind us that the Spirit moves beyond—and in spite of—all the instant knowledge or gratification at our fingertips.

▶ Name some realistic steps we can take toward living upside down, living counterculturally, when it comes to technology and control.

Technology and discernment

▶ If it sounds appealing, brainstorm ideas with a friend for trying out a weekly technology Sabbath or an annual technology-free vacation. Check in with each other on your goals.

▶ Online, we can edit and control what we share about ourselves. Many of us carefully craft and control our online personas through social media photos, updates, and comments. If someone else shaped your online persona solely based on your daily living, would it look different?

3 CAN YOU HEAR ME NOW?
Technology and Community

Scrawled on a piece of yellowed scrap paper and kept on top of our household stack of morning devotion books:

Our Ten Techno-Commandments (in no particular order):

1) Limit screen time after 8 p.m.

2) On any device, pause to respond when spoken to. Look away from the screen!

3) Try not to interrupt a conversation to take a call or check a text.

4) No driving while on the phone. Period.

5) Devices off when visiting or hosting other people.

6) No technology is ever more important than a human being.

7) Real world work and friendships are better than anything virtual or online.

8) If it causes anxiety, not connection, put it away or unplug it.

9) If you can't unplug it over time, put it away or give it away.

10) Check personal email once a week.

Are we idealists? Absolutely. Do we fail at these commandments as imperfect partners, employees, friends, and Christians? On a regular basis. And yet, seeing this list every morning, written in both our handwriting, asks us to at least check in with ourselves and each other about our technology use priorities and hopes from time to time.

> Technology brings more opportunities to engage with communities, both inside and outside our comfort zones. And not just in our social lives.

More and more teleworkers are joining coworking spaces. This means that, for a fee, they can work in an office setting with others who also work remotely.

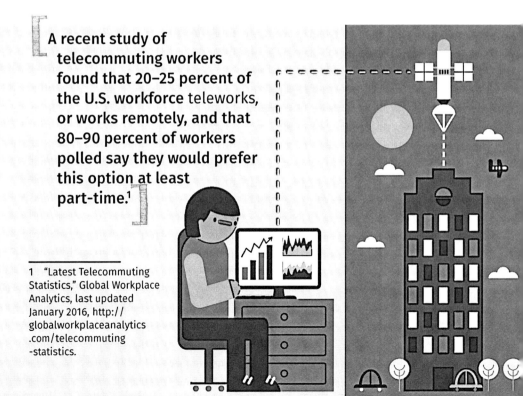

A recent study of telecommuting workers found that 20–25 percent of the U.S. workforce teleworks, or works remotely, and that 80–90 percent of workers polled say they would prefer this option at least part-time.[1]

1   "Latest Telecommuting Statistics," Global Workplace Analytics, last updated January 2016, http://globalworkplaceanalytics.com/telecommuting-statistics.

On many Sunday evenings, my husband and I connect with the congregation where we are members by listening to a recorded podcast of that morning's service. We plug one of our laptops into a set of small speakers that allows us to listen, and, occasionally, we dig out our hymnal and sing along. Or we sit on the couch together with an heirloom family Bible.

Why do we do this? Partly because this congregation is an hour-and-a-half drive away, and we live in a rural part of the state without regular public transportation. We usually only get to be with our faith community in person once a month. We try to make the most of this precious face-to-face time, sharing a meal with different people from the congregation each visit. Throughout the week, we also connect through blog posts from our pastors and a church Facebook page.

Do we feel sad about our limited contributions and relationship-building? Yes. Are we grateful for the ways we can still experience this community because of technology? Absolutely.

When I think about community and faith, the adjective *intentional* immediately comes to mind. For those of us who have lived in a faith-based intentional community, we usually know it's a lot harder than its utopian-sounding description. If only we could choose our housemates, our office mates, our neighbors, and so on!

Many social scientists are saying that, whenever possible, we're beginning to do just that.

> With so many options of how to spend our time and attention, people are opting to connect with communities where they feel most comfortable, both online and off.[2]

According to author and professor Marc Dunkelman, who studies shifts in American communities, during times of crisis in the past (such as the Great Depression), we saw reaching out to those who lived nearby as a necessity and part of our sense of security.

Now, even with ongoing atrocities and crises, many of us don't seem to feel this need as strongly. If we have spare time, we are most likely logging into chat rooms, Skyping family members, or texting friends.

> One-third of Americans today say that they have never met their neighbors.

City planning and transportation planning can also affect who it is we see or live next to. Major highways in my state's largest city have historically divided people by class and race. Traveling to work by vehicle—for roughly 85 percent of Americans, a choice fueled by any number of things, including privilege or lack of reliable choices—means that nearly 75 percent of us are alone in a car during our commute.[3]

---

2   Linda Poon, "Why Won't You Be My Neighbor?" *Atlantic* City Lab, August 19, 2015, http://www.citylab.com/housing/2015/08/why-wont-you-be-my-neighbor/401762/.
3   Emily Badger, "The Lonely American Commute," *Washington Post Wonkblog*, August 14, 2015, https://www.washingtonpost.com/news/wonk/wp/2015/08/14/thelonely-american-commute/.

"For where two or three are gathered

in my name, I am there among them," Jesus says in Matthew 18:20. Today, could *there* even mean Facebook comment threads, Pokémon Go outings, or a packed city bus?

Deuteronomy 15:7 reads, "If there is among you anyone in need, a member of your community in any of your towns within the land that the Lord your God is giving you, do not be hard-hearted or tight-fisted toward your needy neighbor." Because of technology, we are able to aid others on a breathtaking scale. Using lending platforms like Kiva or fundraising sites like GoFundMe, we can support causes around the world, such as microloans in Kenya, adoptions in New Jersey, and girls' schools in Afghanistan.

> Yes, how we define and live out *community* is evolving online, but some would argue we are actually connecting with more strangers, global groups, and social movements.

> Because of technology like live tweeting and hashtags, some of us have grown our awareness and involvement in social justice movements.

Hebrews 10:24-25 says, "Let us consider how to provoke one another to love and good deeds, not neglecting to meet together, as is the habit of some, but encouraging one another." At its best (and our best), technology can help us do just that.

[Talk about It]

Technology and ourselves

▶ How do you define community?

▶ Describe one relationship or community you wouldn't otherwise have without contemporary technology tools.

Technology and others

▶ When do you see technology dividing people the most? What has been a helpful thought or action in these situations?

▶ If you were to write your own set of techno-commandments, what might they be?

▶ Describe a recent situation in which you felt that the other person was completely present with you. How do you practice active listening and being fully present?

Technology and discernment

▶ In your use of daily technology, do you step back to examine whether you are only interacting with communities and ideas that are similar to you or with whom you agree? If not, share your experiences and why you make these choices. If yes, then what could be behind this, and might you be willing to try to break out of this pattern?

▶ Do we put too little or not enough faith in technology as a tool for encouraging or enacting empathy? For social change?

4: TEXTS, TRUTH, AND THE TEMPLE
[Technology and the Body-Mind Connection]

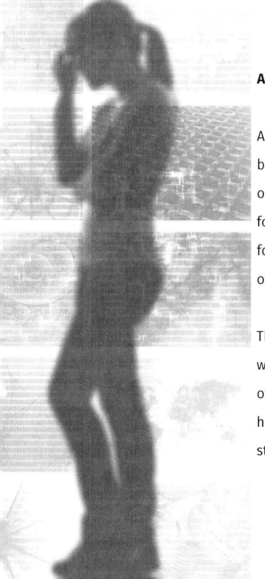

All Day I Let the House

All day I let the house

be filled with voices

on the news. This morning, my body

forgives me

for this extra layer

of violence.

This morning, I leave the house

with a book

of half-read poems,

hold it beside me, my worry

stone.

I wrote this poem after I spent hours listening to live (live!) coverage of the search for Dzhokhar Tsarnaev, better known to many as one of the Boston bombers.

> How do we process this world, and our place within it?

Emotionally, I was completely drained, and I was about to walk into town to teach a class of college students the same age as this young man. I needed something to hold my spirit up; I needed a mentor. For me that day, strength came in the form of poetry as psalm writing, and the mentor whose book I literally carried at my side was World War II conscientious objector William Stafford, who worked four years in Civilian Public Service camps.

If my house is also my body, as many people of faith believe, how do I discern what makes me more godlike, healthier, or more loving?

Technology allows us to make amazing advances in our physical health. From human organs potentially printed by 3-D printers to surgeries that bring back sight or hearing to apps that empower and help those living with migraines, diabetes, Alzheimer's—the list goes on. Medical technologically speaking, there's never been a better time to be living, and living longer.

Go to any major news source, and you'll find more articles and studies than ever before on this topic from healthcare workers, parents, educators, and activists. How we take care of ourselves

> We hear a lot these days about the body-mind connection.

mentally or spiritually can greatly affect our physical health, not only day to day, but also long term. Do we take this seriously?

It might surprise you to learn that Steve Jobs, the late co-founder of Apple, was not secretive about being a low-tech parent. He was intentional about limiting technology use in his home and celebrated a tech-free dinner with his family each night. His children had never played with an iPad.[1] Why? Partly because he and his business partners knew the power of what they were creating and selling.

Jesus still taps us on the shoulder to say, **"Do not worry** about your life, what you will eat or what you will drink, or about your body, what you will wear. Is not life more than food, and the body more than clothing? Look at the birds of the air; they neither sow nor reap nor gather into barns, and yet your heavenly Father feeds them. Are you not of more value than they? And can any of you by worrying add a single hour to your span of life?" (Matthew 6:25-27).

> 1 Corinthians 6:19-20 asks, "Do you not know that your body is a temple of the Holy Spirit within you, which you have from God, and that you are not your own? For you were bought with a price; therefore glorify God in your body."

What might standing have to do with glorifying God? Studies today show alarming health risks attached to our sitting-heavy jobs, transportation choices, and social lives.[2] The good news is that taking regular breaks away from our

---

1   Nick Bilton, "Steve Jobs Was a Low-Tech Parent," *New York Times*, September 10, 2014, http://www.nytimes.com/2014/09/11/fashion/steve-jobs-apple-was-a-lowtech-parent.html?_r=0.
2   Liz Soltan, "Technology and Sitting Too Much," Digital Responsibility, accessed November 10, 2016, http://www.digitalresponsibility.org/technology-and-sitting-too-much/.

screens, meetings, and phone calls to move our bodies can potentially reverse some of the risks.

But we now live in a world where we can work anytime, anywhere. This has drastically affected one of our most basic needs: sleep. Screens that use blue light, like smartphones and tablets, disrupt our sleep patterns, making it more difficult to fall asleep and to get the kinds of sleep needed for optimal rest and renewal. While apps like f.lux adjust screen color past sunset or in early morning to help, the best thing we can do for our physical and mental health is to put away screens after dinner.[3]

On most days I am truly grateful that, no matter the time of day, I can see photos and updates from family, mentors, and friends around the globe because of my phone and laptop and access to high-speed Internet. I have learned that I need to moderate this immersion, however, or else I can't live by one of my favorite sayings, attributed to former U.S. president Teddy Roosevelt: **"Comparison is the thief of joy."** The phrase seems to be a modern take of Jesus' loving message in Matthew 6.

If we are using devices, we also encounter a truly daunting constant flow of advertisements, now reflecting our online search history. We're also presented with definitions of success and beauty and happiness that may clash with how our identity as children of God or as followers of Jesus might define these same things.

Colossians 2:6-7 says, "As you therefore have received Christ Jesus the Lord, continue to live your lives in him, rooted and . . . established in the faith, just as you were taught, abounding in thanksgiving."

---

3   Olga Khazan, "How Smartphones Hurt Sleep," *Atlantic*, February 24, 2105, http://www.theatlantic.com/health/archive/2015/02/how-smartphonesare -ruining-our-sleep/385792/.

[My life is called to reflect the joy of God's peace, grace, and transforming love, and this includes the ways I care for my physical body, mind, and spirit.]

[Talk about It]

Technology and ourselves

▶ Does your current use of technology make it easier or more difficult to "abound in thanksgiving"?

▶ Step back and consider the inner messages that technology plays on repeat during your day or week. What are they?

Technology and others

▶ To improve my health, I started checking personal email once a week and limited Facebook friends to include people I don't get to see in person during a monthlong period. Have you experimented with similar measures, and how successful were you? How did others react?

▶ How have you experienced "Comparison is the thief of joy"? How have others' activities and experiences, many times shared through social media, affected your mental, physical, and spiritual health?

Technology and discernment

▶ How were you raised to think about the body-mind or body-soul connection? What helps you celebrate their connection or union? Singing, praying, or in other ways?

▶ If you work in a job that requires mostly sitting, what are some changes that might allow you to move, like taking walks during meetings or setting alarms that remind you and your office mates to walk outside?

5 ᵒ RIPPLES IN THE WATER
[Technology and Earth Care]

An incomplete portrait of the place I've called home for over a decade:

> Deciduous forests, rock outcroppings, caves, and waterfalls abound—the same **natural beauty** that supports industries like outdoor tourism once attracted the Shawnee and other American Indian tribes who thrived here.

> The local, **slow-food movement** is booming; we host an annual pawpaw festival, many restaurants support local food producers, and we have one of the largest farmers' markets in the country.

> Because of abundant clay and wood to fire kilns, the area was once **world famous** for its locally made bricks. Generations of job opportunities in the fossil fuel extraction trade have also disappeared, leaving behind shrinking and neglected towns, contaminated streams, and an urgent need for new job infrastructure that pays a living wage.

College students flock here by the tens of thousands; sometimes they respect and invest in the community and landscape around them before leaving. Meanwhile, a new generation of back-to-the-landers are starting small farms, solar power companies, and communes—all while the number of oil and gas injection wastewater wells increases.

[**And like any other place, people of faith hold varying beliefs about humanity's ongoing role in the wellness of our planet.**]

In 2015, Pope Francis released a book-length encyclical titled *Laudato Si´: On Care for Our Common Home.* Thanks to the media, Pope Francis's call to repentance and action had an instant global reach. Such a powerful religious leader naming how humanity today has lost touch with God's creation was both shocking and inspiring to many around the world. "We are not God," he wrote. "The earth was here before us and it has been given to us."[1]

---

1   Pope Francis I, "Encyclical Letter *Laudato Si'* of the Holy Father Francis on Care for Our Common Home," May 24, 2015, par. 67, http://w2.vatican.va/content/francesco/en/encyclicals/documents/papa-francesco_20150524_enciclica-laudato-si.html.

This point is echoed in various parts of the Bible, and if we take it seriously, we continue to transform our actions to reflect a sacred connection to our neighbors in creation—all other living things, including plant and animal life.

[**How we define home also influences how we define creation and neighbor.**]

Never before has it been so easy to contact our leaders, or to find ways to plug in (pun very much intended) to environmental education, dialogue, and actions. We can telecommute to meetings and conferences instead of getting in a car or on a plane. Where I live, cutting-edge, infrared research using drones is being used to detect things like water pollution and endangered animal populations, and an app that tracks local buses in real time means more and more people who grew up in rural areas are using public transportation for the first time.

[**Technology can help us in our call to environmental justice and restoration.**]

As climate change affects more of our neighbors—locally, nationally, and halfway around the world—we often hear firsthand accounts because of podcasts, online reporting, or Sunday night Skype talks with missionaries and social justice workers commissioned by our denominations and congregations.

Some weeks, I spend more time looking at digital nature scenes than encountering nature itself. Genesis 2:3 states that God deliberately rested on the seventh day of creating. Perhaps one simple way of honoring God's ongoing artistry would be to truly experience nature every seventh day.

If we don't feel a bond with the natural world, is it easier to take its majesty and wisdom for granted, or to downplay how our choices may affect others now and in the future?

> And yet, technology can also keep us from the natural world, whether from light pollution that hides the stars or from children's outdoor play diminishing.

God spoke: "Let us make human beings in our image, make them reflecting our nature so they can be responsible for the fish in the sea, the birds in the air, the cattle, and, yes, Earth itself, and every animal that moves on the face of Earth." God created human beings; he created them godlike, reflecting God's nature. He created them male and female. God blessed them: "Prosper! Reproduce! Fill Earth! Take charge! Be responsible for fish in the sea and birds in the air, for every living thing that moves on the face of Earth." (Genesis 1:28 *The Message*)

The more technology I use, the more ads I encounter. Luckily, I have a small group of friends who regularly wrestle with linked issues like faith and consumerism. I've learned that an act as simple as walking along the river or weeding a flower bed can reroot me to God's mystery and abundance around me. Farmer and writer Wendell Berry proposes that the interconnectedness of the natural world with other layers of life is more powerful than most of us realize. He writes in his essay "Think Little":

> If we apply our minds . . . to the needs of the earth, then we will have begun to make fundamental and necessary changes in our minds. We will begin to understand and to mistrust and to change our wasteful economy, which markets not just the produce of the earth, but also the earth's ability to produce. We will see that beauty and utility are alike dependent upon the health of the world. But we will also see through the fads and the fashions of protest. We will see that war and oppression and pollution are not separate issues,

but are aspects of the same issue. Amid the outcries for the liberation of this group or that, we will know that no person is free except in the freedom of other persons, and that man's only real freedom is to know and faithfully occupy his place—a much humbler place than we have been taught to think—in the order of creation.[2]

[Talk about It]

Technology and ourselves

▶ How do you define *home*? How is your home's history, present, and future related to the natural world? To environmental justice? If you don't know, do some research online.

▶ Pope Francis writes that "the idea of infinite or unlimited growth, which proves so attractive to economists, financiers and experts in technology . . . is based on the lie that there is an infinite supply of the earth's goods." How does caring for "the earth's goods"[3] fit into your current faith practice? Your use of technology?

Technology and others

▶ I was raised with the saying "Live simply so that others can simply live." How does technology help us to live simply? How does it hinder our living simply?

---

2   Berry, *The Art of the Commonplace: The Agrarian Essays of Wendell Berry* (Counterpoint, 2003), 89.
3   Pope Francis I, *Laudato Si'*, par. 106.

▶ "The more technology I use, the more ads I encounter." Is this statement true for you, too? If so, how do the ads affect your faith? Your consumerism?

Technology and discernment

▶ Research one device you use on a daily basis. What materials is it made of? What company makes this product? Can you find information about the workers who helped make your device? What are their jobs like? What is their quality of life?

▶ How do we find more life in things other than consumerism and materialism in today's world? Personally, I need community and accountability to keep answering this question. I need to cultivate relationships so that possibilities like sharing libraries (where members loan out items instead of buying their own) and time exchanges (where members contribute their talents and resources in equal exchange for needed services and resources—all without exchanging money) feel not only doable but preferable. Would you consider starting a time exchange in your town, or a sharing library with your friends, church, or neighborhood? If so, what things or services would you be interested in sharing?

6: I CAN MAKE PEACE WITH THAT

Technology and 21st-Century Peacemaking

What is your definition of "making peace"?

For some of us, it might mean inviting reconciliation and justice into everyday actions as simple as doing the dishes or listening without judgment. Maybe it means shutting down gossip at work, or learning to mindfully surrender a constant need for control. Peacemaking can have the face of mediation, or humanitarian work in war-torn places. For some people of faith, making peace might even mean supporting military responses to escalating violence.

There are many ideas about how to encourage lasting peace in our world, and more and more of them involve technology use. An evolving PeaceTech movement utilizes technology, data, and media in conflict zones. I believe technology has also further distanced us from our personal role in contemporary warmaking.

> From drones to cyberbullying to Twitter feeds, and from Silicon Valley to technological warfare, we—like generations before us—get to choose how we as Christians engage with the technological advances in our lifetimes.

Theologian Walter Wink frames Jesus' life example as a *third way* to respond to violence, injustice, and our oppressors. Instead of a fight or flight response, Jesus chooses nonviolent resistance—a third way. In parables, relationships, miracles, and even his own death, Jesus topples greater society's assumptions, and challenges an empire's norms.[1]

> If scientific studies and experience show us that the technology we use every day partly feeds on our fight-or-flight human hardwiring, how might we choose a technological third way?

Learning to both tell our own stories and fully listen to others' stories can engage technology in peacemaking steps today. Neither of these actions is passive or easy; they take careful reflection, practice, community, and sometimes risk.

Since 2003, StoryCorps has worked with over one hundred thousand participants to record the largest collection of human stories to date (more than 60,000) for the American Folklife Center at the Library of Congress. The popular radio show's mission is "to preserve and share humanity's stories in order to build connections between people and create a more just and compassionate world."[2] It uses podcasts, animated shorts, an app, and books to share firsthand accounts.

---

1 Walter Wink, "Jesus' Third Way," in *The Powers That Be: Theology for a New Millennium* (New York: Doubleday, 1998), 98–111, available at http://cpt.org/files/BN%20-%20Jesus'%20Third%20Way.pdf.
2 "About," StoryCorps, accessed November 10, 2016, https://storycorps.org/about/.

StoryCorps impact by the numbers

• Increased understanding of people with a disability or serious illness

(96%)

• Increased understanding of immigrants

(95%)

• Increased understanding of Latinos

(94%)

• Increased understanding of African Americans

(91%)

• Strongly agree that StoryCorps makes them feel connected to people with different backgrounds

(88%)

• Reminded listeners of their shared humanity

(81%)

• Helped them see the value in everyone's life story and experience

(80%)

• Humanized social issues, events, and policies

(80%)

• Led listeners to think of people different from themselves as an important part of society

(78%)

• Became interested in thinking about how society could be improved

(71%)

• Made them feel more positive about society

(70%)

Data from the StoryCorps Online Listener Survey collected from nearly 600 listeners between May 2014 and June 2015; and the StoryCorps Radio Listener Survey, conducted for NPR by Lightspeed GMI research in November 2015.

Without these storytelling and sharing resources made possible through electronic tablets, smartphones, and laptops, I believe the knowledge and empathy I need to grow in order to make more third-way decisions would be diminished.

It's hard—if not impossible—to help make peace if we aren't first working towards peace with ourselves and within ourselves. How can we love others if we don't first learn to forgive and welcome our whole selves?

In John 14:27, Jesus assures us of this: "Peace I leave with you; my peace I give to you. I do not give to you as the world gives. Do not let your hearts be troubled, and do not let them be afraid."

What happens when we look through the lens of our technology use to examine this passage?

Ritual can help us transform wounding habits and inner sayings that may reinforce that we are our own worst enemies.

> [Today, the preferred tools to practice rituals often need "on" buttons and chargers.]

Through technology, we can pursue ways to seek, pray, and worship (music, guided meditation, affirmations, poems, and Scriptures) that help us stay connected to the Spirit dancing within, as well as to the holy peering out from every living being.

The next step is making peace with others. Even in families, this can seem like an impossible God-calling—let alone encouraging reconciliation and justice for the poor, refugees, immigrants, lawbreakers, or modern-day Pharisees among us.

Perhaps we can talk the talk, but walking in the footprints of peace means a risk and sacrifice we aren't ready to make. Imagine the voice of God calling us out in this manner:

> Quit your worship charades.
>   I can't stand your trivial religious games:
> Monthly conferences, weekly Sabbaths, special
>   meetings—
>   meetings, meetings, meetings—I can't stand one more!
>
>   You've worn me out!
> I'm sick of your religion, religion, religion,
>   while you go right on sinning.
> When you put on your next prayer-performance,
>   I'll be looking the other way.
> No matter how long or loud or often you pray,
>   I'll not be listening.

And do you know why? Because you've been tearing
  people to pieces, and your hands are bloody.
Go home and wash up.
  Clean up your act.
Sweep your lives clean of your evildoings
  so I don't have to look at them any longer.
Say no to wrong.
  Learn to do good.
Work for justice.
  Help the down-and-out.
Stand up for the homeless.
  Go to bat for the defenseless.

—Isaiah 1:13-17 (*The Message*)

While we are likely more comfortable concentrating on the second part of this passage—a go-get-'em call to action—its passionate accusation and call to accountability still surely stings with truth.

Some positive news: because of technological advances like social media, we are—right now—helping to stop human trafficking (truckersagainsttrafficking.org), poverty (kiva.org), cyberbullying (teachpeacenow.com), hunger (unsung.org and freerice.com), street harassment (ihollaback.org), and much, much more.

> So how can we live out the parable of the good Samaritan in a world where we're so intensely "connected alone," where technology can enable things like unchecked privilege or individualism?

> Perhaps the most important leap in our contemporary third-way living is to constantly look for ways of growing our faith and experiencing God's heart in our online and offline communities.

[Talk about It]

Technology and ourselves

▶ What technologies help you feel more connected to your faith family and to peacemaking?

▶ What stories or perspectives might be missing from your understanding of your neighborhood, nation, and world? How might you use technology to conscientiously seek those out?

Technology and others

▶ In what ways do you witness technology being a positive step forward in contemporary peacemaking?

▶ Awareness and education can be important layers to making long-lasting peace. Consider using a device to read or listen to holy books from another tradition, which are available online. Pay special attention to the teachings regarding peace and violence.

Technology and discernment

▶ If, through things like scientific studies and experience, we know that phones and other devices feed on our tendency to choose a fight-or-flight option, how might we choose a technological, Jesus-inspired third way—one that doesn't necessarily reject most technology, for instance?

▶ If you aren't familiar with the websites named in this session, look them up and read more about their missions. Do you utilize other websites and apps to encourage peace ripples?

▶ In a small group, rewrite the parable of the good Samaritan (Luke 10:25-37) and insert different characters and technologies to tell a modern-day version that reflects the role technology plays in your lives.

[About the Writer]

Becca J. R. Lachman considers herself a stumbling Anabaptist and a recovering creative writing degree collector. Raised in Kidron, Ohio, she has lived since 2005 in the foothills of the Appalachian Mountains in Athens, Ohio, with her husband, Michael. Over the last decade, she has taught college students, coordinated writing centers, and written speeches for university administrators. Currently, she works as the communications officer for her county's vibrant, seven-branch public library system—a job that takes her to community festivals in former coal towns, story times featuring baby goats, and intergenerational tango classes. Becca and her husband are grateful to be members of Columbus Mennonite Church.

You can find Becca's poems and essays in places such as *Image, Brevity, Consequence Magazine, Ohio Today, On Being*'s blog, *Timbrel, the Mennonite,* and more. Her poetry books include *The Apple Speaks* and *Other Acreage,* and she edited the poetry anthology *A Ritual to Read Together: Poems in Conversation with William Stafford.*

CPSIA information can be obtained
at www.ICGtesting.com
Printed in the USA
FFOW03n0742170117
31312FF